How to edit a novel

CHARLOTTE NASH

About the author

Charlotte Nash is the author of four Australian small-town romances: bestselling *Ryders Ridge*, *Iron Junction*, *Crystal Creek*, and *The Horseman*; and speculative fiction short stories, including three short-listed for the Aurealis and Ditmar awards. She has degrees in engineering and medicine, and her work as an engineer brings project management experience to novel editing. She is currently a PhD candidate at The University of Queensland, where she also teaches manuscript editing in some semesters. charlottenash.net | charlienash.net

CONTENTS

Introduction

I wrote this book because when I was a very early career writer, I found lots of information about what might be wrong with my novel, but very little on *how* to convert that knowledge into edits on the page. Over time, I developed an approach that was methodical, thorough, and, importantly, let me know when my novel edit was done. It also turned editing for me from something I hated into something I love.

It surprised me when I started teaching that most writers weren't using a method for their own edits. Someone once told me that writers are generally unorganised – I don't believe that, but if you're not approaching your edit with some method, the odds of failure (including just not finishing) are high.

I'm not going to waste your time with a long introduction. You want to get to editing. So, what follows are five steps that I've acronymed PAPER. Do the steps in order. Heed the advice, and edit your novel properly so it can go where you intend (self-publish, agent or publisher submission) in the best shape possible. Good luck.

Before you start

The PAPER method stands for:

- P – Preparation
- A – Analysis
- P – Planning
- E – Execution
- R – Review

A glossary of terms is in Appendix A, and one-page summary of the whole process is given in Appendix B. Before moving to Preparation, please read the few things below so you don't get lost.

The editing hierarchy

Many early-career writers think that editing is making sentences nicer. This is a huge mistake, and will waste your time. Editing exists in a hierarchy as follows:

- Structural editing – addresses the story-level issues, such as plot, character, narrative structure, setting, tone, consistency, and other 'big-picture' issues.
- Copyediting – addresses sentence-level expression, such as word choice, sentence style and structure, and consistency of small details.
- Proofreading – checking for errors in spelling, grammar and typography only.

They always, ALWAYS, go in order, and the PAPER method is mostly about structural editing, which is the one that makes the most improvement, but is often hardest to manage. Copyediting and proofreading are covered in the 'Review' step.

Editing is hard at first, but it gets easier

The first time you edit properly (using PAPER or any other method) it's likely to feel daunting, difficult or frustrating. This is normal. Persist. It gets better each time, and you'll begin to achieve a mastery where you can combine steps and adapt them to your individual style. To help align your expectations, I've provided a guide for how long different writing and editing tasks take me in Appendix H. I consider myself still an early-career writer, with about 10 years' experience all up.

The synergistic thinking needed to write or edit – thinking about the interplay of characters, plot, rhythm, setting, and themes, etc. – is not simple. The only way to gain the skills is to engage with the craft, over and over. Be critiqued. Edit your own work. Edit other people's work. Read, and watch narrative, and think about what you're reading and watching. Slowly, skills will build, and editing will feel more natural.

The writer's caveat

Writers should view anyone who says 'this is the only way to do X' with a high degree of suspicion. PAPER is my method, and may or may not work for you. PAPER is a good place to start, however, even if you end up changing it to suit yourself.

Back up your work

If your precious manuscript is not backed up (and I mean *automatically*, at least every day, to an external hard-drive or the cloud) then STOP RIGHT NOW AND SORT THAT OUT. I've known writers who lost their whole manuscript and had to start again. I've had hard-drive failures myself and lost months of work. Go get a free Dropbox account and sync your writing documents there, at the very least. I sync all my writing documents to the cloud, and also back up my hard-drive every day.

The final warning

DO NOT fuss around with your sentences until you have structurally edited. Many a writer has fallen under the wheels of their own desire to meddle, spending hours finessing prose or dialogue that later needs to be cut. All that effort just makes the cut harder, with gnashing of teeth, or worse – bending the story to fit your prose and not the other way around. If you are in the habit of fixing your sentences as the first thing you do when editing, stop. Do whatever you have to do to break the habit – work on paper, think of editorial hit men who'll break your fingers, whatever. But put your pen down and back away.

Step 1 – Preparation

Prepare your editing tools

About this step

Preparation gives you a "big-picture" view of your novel and creates all the tools you will need. This is to avoid feeling as if you have a huge nebulous task in front of you, and to ensure the manuscript is ready to be edited. Ideally, this step happens after the manuscript has been rested (at least a month is good, I think).

What you need

- Your manuscript
- A paper notebook, spreadsheet, or other place to record your *scene list*

What you'll produce

- A *scene list* and *time map*
- Your story's metadata (optional)
- A cleanly formatted manuscript, ready for editing.

PREPARATION – Steps to complete

Read the manuscript to create the scene list and time map

A *scene list* (and *time map*) are absolutely essential. Examples are shown in Appendix C. These two tools give you:

- A condensed summary of your novel
- An index for editing

- A quick way to look for problems with repetition, pace problems, settings, and more (when we get to Analysis).

To create the **scene list**, read through the novel from beginning to end, writing down a summary of each scene. Your task is to capture the novel as it really is. You can make notes about things you want to change, but do it separately. DO NOT CHANGE ANYTHING. Do this step even if you made a scene plan when you were writing, because what was planned probably isn't exactly what's on the page. You can create your scene list in hard copy, in a table in a word processing document, in a spreadsheet (my preference), or whatever works for you.

Here's the minimum information I record for each scene:

- Chapter number and scene letter (I use numbers for chapters, and letters for scenes, so '3a' means the first scene in chapter 3).
- Point-of-view character.
- Scene summary (keep it short: one or two sentences about what happens, capturing the character and conflict, such as: *Mary interrogates Josh about his relationship with Vera. She knows he's lying.*).

You can record other things depending on the type of book you have and what you want to know, such as:

- Setting (where the scene takes place)
- Time/date (I keep a separate timeline of scenes which is the **time map** described below, because timing/chronology is its own problem and I prefer to see it graphically)
- What subplots are involved in the scene (I often just make a column for each subplot, and place an X in it if that scene is relevant to the subplot)
- Word count

At the same time, create a **time map**. This is a summary of where all the scenes take place in time. I use the scene numbers to make it easy. For example, if my book takes place over four months, I have four months of a calendar (maybe just made with a ruler in my notebook) with the scenes (1a, 13b, 22e, etc.) written on the appropriate days – at the top of the box for the morning, at the bottom for night, you get the idea. You can construct whatever time representation you need, such as making breaks in a calendar for longer novels. Laying it out in one place is superb for:

- checking cross-references in the novel to when earlier events occurred
- avoiding continuity problems when inserting new scenes or moving scenes
- checking days of the week, moon phases, and other time-dependent facts.

Once you have the scene list and time map, preparation is almost done.

Compile manuscript metadata

I consider this step as optional, because I often don't do it in my edit now, or I combine it with Analysis. The idea is to do some high-level thinking about your manuscript, making sure there's no big blunders in how your story comes across to the reader. Later, the Review step will cover pitches, blurbs and synopses, and this metadata will be relevant again there. After creating the scene list, you should be able to answer the following questions.

What is your genre?

Or perhaps a better question: what kind of story will the reader expect? Most writers understand broadly about "genre" – that we are writing thriller, crime, romance, literary, or some combination. Those genre labels are mostly about how a book is marketed. Right now, this step cares more about the reader – what expectations are set for them through the genre hints in your opening pages, and what promise is the book making about the story?

If you haven't thought of books this way, take down two or three favourites from your bookshelf now. Look at the first page. What indications are present as to the genre and type of story? Examine the language, the characters and the situation. For instance, a crime novel may begin with the discovery of a body.

Example – establishing genre

Good examples that I often use in classes are listed below. If you have any of these stories, look at the elements I note in the first page that gives the reader a firm idea of what to expect.

Snow Crash by Neal Stephenson. Genre: cyberpunk. Look at the language and rhythm of the opening, and the urban setting. The story promises high concepts and dramatic action.

Lover Avenged by J R Ward. Genre: urban fantasy / erotic romance. The mash up of old-world language and symbols is contrasted with modern slang and real-world references. The story promises a power struggle to be resolved.

Temeraire: Throne of Jade by Naomi Novik. Genre: historical fantasy. The language and setting gives us the strong impression of historical fiction, but reference to a Chinese embassy in Europe in the era of Napoleon hints at fantasy. (The stylised dragon also gives this away).

Why is this important? Defeated expectations are a problem for readers. If you story comes across as a detective tale, but there's no crime in the first half of the book, that's a problem. If you've written a romance, but you have an unhappy ending, or the couple don't meet until halfway through, that could be a problem. If your story reads like a historical saga, but aliens turn up on page 100 without any signal that might happen, that could be a problem.

Genre expectations also play into word length. A high-fantasy epic may be acceptable over 150,000 words, but a YA novel usually won't exceed 80,000. Make an effort to find out the length expectations for your genre, especially if you have a publisher in mind. If your novel is wildly outside the common lengths for your genre, maybe you've written more than one book, or maybe you need to edit to substantially reduce (or add to) your word count.

Looking at these issues now can be really important, because if you have one of these issues, it's easier to fix it in the edit, rather than afterwards.

What other similar titles are out there?

Avoid saying *A Game of Thrones*, *Harry Potter*, *Twilight* or anything else that is a redonkulously successful outlier of publishing. You want to be able to answer this question with 2 – 4 similar genre/readership titles that are good sellers (or well regarded in some other way, such as awards) but that show you have read other things in your genre besides the stonkingly successful titles currently occupying pop-culture. If you don't know this yet, okay, but eventually you'll need to know. Disregard this if you are not planning to publish.

What is your point of difference?

Looking at your similar-titles answer, how is your story identifiable amidst the pack? What do you have that they don't? Again, disregard if you are not planning to publish.

Write down the answers to these questions, and hold them in mind as you go through the other PAPER steps. They'll come in handy for the Review stage.

Format your manuscript

I believe strongly in proper formatting from the start – it makes your job easier. Formatting should be invisible so the work stands for itself, and failing to follow the accepted rules of formatting can leave a poor impression. If you use Scrivener or other programs to manage your formatting, fine, but you don't need to use a program like that.

Here are the two golden rules of formatting:

- If the publisher or agent has guidelines, use those. Follow them absolutely.
- If no guidelines are given, use 'industry standard' formatting:
  - 3 cm margins (2.5 cm at absolute minimum)
  - Times New Roman font, 12pt
  - Double line spacing, and no extra spacing after paragraphs
  - Plain headings. Use the same font as for the text and use bold (and larger size, if desired) to indicate the heading.
  - Indent 1 cm at the beginning of each paragraph. More looks funny, less is hard to see where new paragraphs begin

o Use either a large white space, or a symbol on a new line (# or ***) to show scene breaks. If you use a white space, don't indent the first paragraph of the next scene. If you use a symbol, you can choose whether or not to indent.

o Headers/footers – put nothing in the footer. The header should be: aligned left: About XXX words; aligned right: Author Surname / Book Title / Page No. First page headers can be different and include your contact information aligned left, with the approximate word count aligned right, then the other pages are as above.

A summary of this guide is included in Appendix D, along with a link to a YouTube video showing you how to set up Microsoft Word to do this automatically.

Summary

To conclude, Preparation ensures your tools are in order. Before you move on to Analysis:

- Complete a clean read of your manuscript, compiling the scene list and time map.
- Identify your genre, other similar works, and what makes this book stand out (optional).
- Format your manuscript to industry standards.

Step 2 – Analysis

Work out what to fix in your manuscript

About this step

Analysis is where you work out what needs to change in the manuscript (the issues, problems, or broken bits). Analysis is done by looking at the **scene list**, **time map**, and the manuscript itself. Many aspects will require all three and, of course, knowledge of writing craft.

What you need

- Your **scene list** and **time map**
- Your manuscript
- A paper notebook, or somewhere else to write down your **problem list**.

What you'll produce

- A **problem list** – a rough, raw list of issues with the story.

Before you start

General notes

This book is about the editing process. It does not cover the massive breadth of craft information needed to understand problems in a manuscript – there're many other books out there for that. Here, I'm assuming that you either have those skills already, or that you are working with a report from your publisher, manuscript assessor, or knowledgeable beta reader (you are going to do your own Analysis, but someone else's notes are gold for guidance).

If you have none of those things, stop. If you haven't edited before, consider paying for a structural report from a recommended editor. Otherwise, the days and weeks of work you're about to embark on could be severely misguided. Seeing through your own work is extremely difficult – this improves with experience, but you'll never have the perspective an external party can provide. You should have your own ideas, but be prepared to confront some issues you haven't seen, and they may be big.

Here are some ways to identify a good structural editor:

- They come recommended by someone with some authority in the business (published author, working editor, publisher).
- They provide a fixed-price quote for a reasonable amount
- They can show you a sample of their previous work
- They treat you with respect, and are punctual with communication.

Poor choices of structural editors:

- People who are related to you
- People who can't show you any evidence of previous work
- People who are offering a cut-price deal. You get what you pay for.
- People who correct your spelling or grammar. This is not structural editing, and a proper structural editor knows it.

As you embark on Analysis, here are some critical things to remember:

- Avoid dwelling on how to solve the problems (which is the goal of the next step – Planning). If you think of ideas, keep a record of them with the problem they relate to, but focus on understanding the problems. One step at a time. Better solutions often present themselves when you can see all the problems as a whole.
- Do not 'fix as you go', even if the issue appears to be a small and easy thing to remedy. Problems in novels are usually interconnected. Later may come a better idea that solves more than one problem, or you might inadvertently create new problems with premature fixing.
- Distance yourself from your work as much as possible. This is where resting the manuscript, and feedback from a beta reader or

professional editor can really help. You must be prepared to let go of your preconceptions about your story.

Example

My second novel, *Iron Junction*, started out with a back-story between the two main characters, where they had known each other as teenagers. The first feedback I got from a trusted editor identified this as a problem for the story, and suggested it be cut. But I doggedly hung onto the idea, thinking it would be hard to remove and trying other fixes to make it "work". It didn't, and I finally saw the light late in my structural edit with the publisher many months later. In fact, this back-story was super easy to remove and solved a bunch of problems – only my preconception about the story stopped me from saving myself all that trouble.

About the problem list

The ***problem list*** is the critical output of *Analysis*, and this is my suggestion on how to lay it out. You may refine or change it to suit yourself.

- Keep the list separate to your manuscript (though it's fine to mark up places where issues are apparent on the manuscript itself). The easiest way to do this is to use a notebook or spreadsheet. You may want to divide your page into two columns (problems on the left, relevant scenes or other notes on the right), or simply make bullet points and write location/note information underneath each point. The reason the list needs to be separate is that you need to think of your problems and fixes in a group (rather than being attached to isolated pages of your manuscript).
- Note at least the following information:
    - A description of the problem, such as: *John's reaction to Belinda's betrayal not believable – too passive.* Or, *plot logic – If John calls Nerida first, why would he trust Teresa more than Nerida later?*
    - Where you find the problem (scene number, such as 4c, 5b) – this comes in handy later when we work out a strategy for fixing the issues. If you don't know at this

point (i.e. it's a large, overarching problem), that's fine. Working out where to fix it is also part of Planning.

o   Whether the problem falls into a category, such as *John's character or Subplot – Nerida's secret*. Again, this helps when drawing together the list later, but isn't essential.

o   Some indication of how important you think the issue is to the story overall. Some issues will have a large impact, others won't. Use stars, perhaps, to indicate the big issues. This helps you to prioritise the list later.

ANALYSIS – Steps to complete

If you are working with a structural report, use that as a basis for your **problem list**, and add anything else that you note in the steps below. If you don't have a structural report, and don't trust your own skills in this area, I have provided some basic questions to consider in Appendix E.

1.   First, examine the **scene list** and **time map**, writing down any problems (and any obvious corresponding scenes) in your **problem list**. Remember to add any problems you noted when you were creating the scene list and time map.
2.   Next, read through the manuscript, adding any further problems to the list. Remember not to change anything yet.

Summary
To conclude, the point of Analysis is to work out what needs to change in your draft manuscript by examining your **scene list** and your actual manuscript using your knowledge of narrative craft. Before you move on to Planning, record all the structural issues with your novel in one place, the **problem list**.

Step 3 – Planning

Plan what you will change, and where

About this step

Planning develops a plan for the edit that you can then systematically execute.

For me, this chapter (and the next) is stuff I rarely see taught. Lots of professional development for writers focuses on manuscript problems and how to solve them in principle, but often in a big-picture way. Just as a synopsis is not a novel, knowing that *the villain needs to be stronger* is not telling you what scenes to change and how. And that's what we really have to do when editing.

Planning is where many edits fall down – knowing what's wrong with your story is not enough. Insight doesn't equal change – you need a plan. Planning when writing helps you manage your 'off' days, and planning in editing does the same. Planning also helps to show how the issues are connected.

Note

If, after doing the Analysis, you feel that the manuscript is in very bad shape (by which I mean that major sections need re-organising, re-writing, or plots or major characters are completely changing), there's an alternative way to attack the edit, which is to re-write. I have done this twice – once where I needed to re-write about 20,000 words to completely change the sequence of some events and which characters were involved; and another where I needed to re-write nearly half the book – in the first case, I did this as part of a larger plan as described in this section. In the second, I re-wrote the whole book instead.

So, a re-write can either replace the edit, or fix large sections before going onto other structural issues. To plan a re-write, I suggest the following:

- Write a new scene list for the sections (or for the whole book) describing what the scenes need to be to fix the problems.

- Map across any relevant material in the existing manuscript (that is, identify the existing scene numbers that you can draw from).

- Re-write scenes as needed, in order from the beginning of the novel to the end.

- If you re-wrote part of the novel, go back to Preparation and ensure your *scene list* and *time map* are accurate, then review your Analysis to check it's still accurate, and proceed then to the rest of this Planning step for other issues that aren't in the re-written parts. If you re-wrote the whole book, go onto Review.

I don't suggest doing this unless things are in a bad way. Be prepared that substantial re-writes often require another edit, though perhaps less extensive than for a first draft.

What you need
- Your problem list
- A paper notebook, or spreadsheet, or somewhere else to make your editing plan.

What you'll produce
- Your *editing plan* (and example to refer to is in Appendix G)

PLANNING – Steps to complete

Group your problems

The first task is always to organise the **problem list** into something more meaningful that you can work with. Every writer will do this a little differently, and there's no prescription. You may make one broad issue called "plot", then have a number of sub-issues that are all to do with plot. Such as "the way Christina finds out about John seems implausible", "the resolution is incomplete – we never find out what happens to Harriet". Or, you could just make those two separate points. I tend to group character problems all together under that character, and make separate items for relationships between characters, for plot items, and other structural problems. But each edit (and editor) will organise this differently - I don't believe it matters much how, so long as you do organise the problems - doing so forms a complete picture of the issues in your mind.

Some issues will overlap (for example, motivation for characters' actions can be as much a "character" issue as a "plot" one) but this doesn't matter. As long as the groupings make sense to you, this will be fine.

You may also find you have solutions or "semi-solutions" listed as problems. For example, "Make Greta more likeable" or "Change Raymond's childhood experience with his father". If you do, make sure you think back to what actual problem that solution was trying to address. This makes it easier to think more broadly about solutions.

Tip

Most stories have issues both large and small, and all sizes in between. Not all those issues matter equally: some will have a large influence of the story quality, and some won't. When you organise your problems, identify the issues that you think have the largest bearing on making the story better. You don't have to put them at the top, but recognise that finding solutions to those problems is more important than the others.

So, what do you actually need to do? I take a notebook, and open to a double-page spread. I write down the problems on the left-hand side of the page, leaving each a large gap (I fit only 2 or 3 per page – the space is for working notes). I number the problems 1, 2, 3, etc., as I go. Leave the right side of the double page blank – this is for the solutions.

Solve the problems

So, now you have half your editing plan – all the organised problems. Great. Now all you have to do is solve them. Easy, right? I hear you all laughing. Solving problems can be an art, and some of us are better at it than others. Before you start, remember solutions must be:

- *Specific.* This means it must tell you what you're changing. A vague idea like "make a character stronger" could mean anything. However, "change George's responses to his mother so he deflects her jibes and protects others from them" is highly specific, and you understand clearly what needs to change. Non-specific solutions will hamstring you when you come to looking at the manuscript, so be as specific as possible about what you'll change.
- *Directed.* This means the solution actually targets the problem you're trying to solve. Sometimes if you have a cool idea, it's just that – a cool idea that doesn't do anything for the problem.
- *Compatible.* This means that you can actually achieve the solution in the story – that the scenes exist (or can be created) to implement the solution, and it's not at odds with the story's tone, genre or spirit. For example, if you want to solve a problem of villain motivation, but your novel is written in another character's perspective, adding a scene in the villain's POV might come across as odd. You may have to consider instead giving them a number of scenes, or seeing how motivation could be implied by actions the viewpoint character can observe.

So now understanding what a solution needs to be, here are some methods to come up with solutions. As you do so, you should know your problems well enough by now to recognise where a solution might take care of more than one problem. These are the golden moments in editing.

- *Use a prompt list.* A list of some fixes for particular problems is given in Appendix F. This is my least favourite way to solve problems, but reading through the list can add to your own internal pool of problem fixes.

- *Discussion with a buddy.* Someone else will always have different ideas, you just need to trust yourself to evaluate their suggestions. This is my favourite way to solve problems – talking about your issue out loud to someone else may be all you need to do, and the process is fun with a supportive listener.
- *Comparison.* Can you identify a similar situation you've seen done well in another narrative? Could you use a similar idea? For instance, I've had the problem of low sexual tension between two characters. So, I re-read a bunch of stories where I thought sexual tension was really well done. I was then able to see that I could fix one book by changing the characters' back-story (to increase anticipation) and another book simply needed deeper descriptions of passion. This is why reading and paying attention to narrative is so useful.
- *Past experience.* Have you had this problem before? How did you solve it? Could that work again?
- *Professional input.* An extension on the buddy discussion, a professional editor will think about solutions, and a structural report should contain specific ideas on how to solve the problems. It doesn't always make them right, but their suggested solution can help you understand the problem more deeply.

As I come up with solutions, I write them underneath the problem on the left-hand side of the double page. Use the **scene list** and **time map** as you go to check timings, dates and continuity. Many problems may have only one solution; others might require a few changes. Again, leave some room between each one. You may prefer to generate all the solutions before you make the final editing plan, so that you don't have to guess at the spacing.

Tip

While solutions come in all different forms, there's a couple of changes I suggest thinking carefully about, because they represent hours and hours of work.

- **Changing tense**. If you have written in the past-tense, and want more immediacy, you may think that writing in the present tense would work better. This is enormous work. Tense changes are rarely a simple case of changing

---

all the verbs (and even that is massive in a manuscript of 100,000 words) – the rhythms and expressions of one tense do not neatly translate into another. If you are considering a tense change, think carefully whether you could do something else. The expression can usually be improved to make the tense work. Any editor who suggests a tense change like this to a writer deserves some kind of punishment.

- **Changing POV from first to third, and vice versa.** It's not uncommon to change the point-of-view in individual scenes. This happens for one or two scenes in every book I write. But changing an entire manuscript from third to first person (or first to third) is a massive undertaking. As for tense changes, the perspective does not easily translate, and effectively means re-writing the text. I have known writers who have done this, chiefly because they couldn't 'connect' with a character in one tense, but could in another. But this is not a change to make lightly.

Map solutions into the manuscript

So, now you have a usable list of solutions to an organised list of problems. One thing left to do – map the solutions into the manuscript. Generally, there are three types of solutions:

- Insert new material
- Delete existing material
- Change existing material

Sometimes, your solutions may require a combination. For example, in a recent structural edit, I had to:

- Insert a new subplot involving the protagonist's mother (involved a few new scenes, and additions to existing scenes)
- Delete three minor characters (required a change of events in several scenes to achieve the same outcomes without those characters)
- Change a bullying scene to make interactions less schoolyard and more adult (deletions and additions to the same scene).

Regardless of which type of solution you have, this is how I map the solution into the manuscript:

- Work now on the right-hand side of your double-page spread. Against each of the problems on the left, write your specific solution on the right. For this, record both:
  - o **What** is being inserted/deleted/changed. You may need to devote several lines if you need to make notes about what a few new scenes are.
  - o **Where** to make the change. Use your scene list to identify all the scenes that you think will be affected by a change. For instance, if you need to insert a subplot, what new scenes will you add, and where? Which existing scenes will you add to or change?
- As you do this, consider knock-ons. You may create other issues in making changes, both negative and positive. Especially, consider:
  - o Your time continuity – have you mucked it up by inserting, deleting or changing events? (use your *time map*)
  - o Conflicts – have you created inconsistencies with existing material? If so, does that require a further change?
  - o Reinforcements – can you actually use the new material to strengthen what you already have? For example, can you add to a theme, or tie in with an existing subplot?
- You may realise from this that you may get to considering knock-ons and realise that the solution isn't going to work for the story. The problem-solving stage can therefore become iterative, going back to look at other solutions. This is why is it extremely important not to change anything until you have a complete list of solutions!

Summary

The critical points of Planning are to complete your plan before you change anything, making sure your solutions work for the problem, and then map solutions to specific scenes in your book. Before you move on to Execution:

- Ensure your list of problems is grouped or organised in a way that works for you.

- Come up with specific, directed and compatible solutions for each problem.
- Map all the problems you've solved onto the manuscript, identifying specific scenes where elements need to be inserted, deleted or changed. When this is done, you have your ***editing plan***.

You can organise the ***editing plan*** any way you want, but I work in a paper notebook organised like this:

- On the left side of a double-page spread, list the problem area and the solutions (or what needs to change) underneath.
- On the right side, I list the scenes that need changes for each item, and any related notes.
- I leave lots of room to add extra notes, and scribble things as I'm going. I keep my time map and scene list separate, and on paper.

Step 4 – Execution

Perform the edit

About this step

If you have all the tools, the editing process is reasonably straightforward. That doesn't mean it's easy. This section will address both doing the work of the edit, and how to manage yourself doing it. "Editor's avoidance" is the equivalent of "writers block" – both are easier to manage with a plan, and need to be managed if you want to get the job done.

What you'll need

- Your *scene list* and *time map*
- Your *editing plan*
- Your formatted manuscript.

What you'll produce

- A structurally editing manuscript, ready for copyediting.

EXECUTION – Steps to complete

Rank the edit list

One thing I do before starting is to look at each item on the editing plan and rank it – "Easy", "Medium" or "Hard". There's no rules on how I decide, I just look at the problem, and go with my gut feeling on how much effort that's going to take (time, or pain and suffering) to put into the manuscript. Do the same for your list – the reason why is later.

Do the work

The idea now is simply to attack the list. You know how you will solve the problem, and where to go in the manuscript to do it, so just be systematic. You don't have to start at the beginning, but there may be a natural order to the problems. For example, you might want to write in a new subplot first, so that you can bear this in mind when making other changes. But I recommend for any one solution, to work through the affected scenes from beginning to the end of the manuscript. This helps with continuity.

Don't worry if you think you might be missing things (because you will). You will probably make minor stuff-ups in timing, and miss references to things that you delete or change. Those things you'll fix in Review. I think of it this way: structural editing is like the power tool phase of woodwork – you just want to get all the shapes roughly right. In Review, you take out the sandpaper and refine. So don't drive yourself mad looking for every tiny reference. That conversation buried in chapter 20 where a one-line mention is made of something you deleted in scene five? That will be found later.

All that remains is to do your edit. Cross off each item as you finish it, and update your *scene list* and *time map* as you go in case you need to come back. When everything is crossed off, you're done!

Tip

If you are adding scenes, it's useful to use a different scene number in your *scene list* and *time map* while you are working. For instance, if adding a scene after scene 5b (second scene in chapter 5), you might call this "5b1" especially if 5c already exists. This allows you to update the *time map* without altering all the scene numbers, and preserves the mapping of your solutions. You can renumber all the scenes in both list and map when the edit is finished.

Managing yourself through the edit

As with writer's block, it's easy to procrastinate or avoid doing your edit. Acknowledge there will be times (maybe many) where you won't want to do the work. Unfortunately, if you're a professional, you have deadlines.

Everyone has practical constraints (work, children, pets, spouses) on writing and editing, but they can be overcome. Here are some strategies for overcoming the avoidance.

- *Use the ranking system.* When your mood for editing is poor, go to the items you've marked "Easy" – crossing something off with less effort can be enough to get you back in the mood, and in the practice of being in your chair. When you're having a stellar day, go for "Hard" ones.
- *Turn off your critic.* You suck. Everything sucks. The critic comes out most acutely when you're wrestling with a hard problem and everything seems stupid and dumb and is never going to work. Examine the true motivation – is it just hard? Or are you losing faith in the solution? If it's the latter, you may need to revisit it. The former, you'll need to employ the same tricks as when writing – remember it will pass, that everyone goes through this, that no one ever has to read it if you don't want them to, or convince yourself you'll just fix one issue in one scene.
- *Apportion time.* If you're time-poor, a well-constructed plan will help. You can choose something small when you only have limited time to use. My second-most recent edit was achieved on weekends and evenings while working a full-time job, and editing someone's thesis. My most recent one was done with a four-month-old baby at home and no childcare.
- *Deadlines.* Never underestimate their ability to motivate.
- *Support.* When you're really low, reach out to your fellow writers for encouragement. Everyone's been there. Try to find a flesh and blood person, but go to social media if you have to. And if you're distracted by those platforms, consider internet blocking software such as Freedom or Anti-Social to keep yourself on task.

Summary

Execution is the big workload of the edit – where you actually make the changes. Before you move on to Review:

- Firstly rank your edits from easy to hard.

- Then, go through the problems systematically, changing the manuscript scenes and crossing off items in the *editing plan* as they're done.
- Throughout, manage yourself to stay on task when motivation wanes.

Step 5 – Review

Clean up and prepare your manuscript for submission

About this step

This final step may be more familiar ground when you think about editing – improving expression, fixing spelling mistakes, things that basically involve starting at the beginning of the manuscript and editing as you go. In PAPER, Review is the last step after the structural edit is done. It's the clean-up: you catch things you missed, perform a copyedit, and also prepare the project for submission.

What you'll need

- Your structurally edited manuscript
- Any resources you like for copyediting – such as a style manual or dictionary.

What you'll produce

- Your finished manuscript
- Any other materials for submission – blurb, synopsis and/or cover letter.

REVIEW – Steps to complete

Clean read, and copyedit

Once you've completed the structural edit, your first task is to "clean read" the book. This means to read it from beginning to end. You've just made a bunch of changes, and you need to make sure that the story still gels together, and whether any issues, like continuity, have been missed.

You can also now (finally) do a copyedit (improving the expression at the sentence level). At first, you may want to split these tasks into two – clean read once first, looking for any lingering issues and appreciating the story as a whole, and then read again doing the copyedit, where you'll have to pay attention at a closer level. Once you've done this a few times, you can combine them.

You can choose how you like to work – mark up on paper (which can make it easy to read twice, but only transfer changes once), or make changes direct in the electronic copy – either way, keep a copy of all versions. Once those changes are made, you are done.

Copyediting skills
Again, this book is about the process of the edit, and doesn't go into the very specific skill set that copyediting requires. A good copyeditor needs to understand and consider basic issues like:

- Dialogue, including attributions, natural speech, and beats
- Verb choice
- Clichés
- Repetition of words and phrases
- Padding phrases
- Weak amplifiers
- Overwriting
- Mixed metaphors

... as well as a sense for expression and style consistent with the novel. In addition, they need to fix minor inconsistencies in details (such as character ages, or physical descriptions) and ensure consistency in the choice of spelling, hyphenation and capitalisation. Copyediting is a specialist skill that all writers should foster in themselves, but if you know you're not strong in this area, you can pay someone to do it for you.

If you're copyediting yourself, here are some suggestions on the process:

- Try to clear time for copyediting so that you do it in large blocks. It's easier to spot continuity problems that way (e.g. a blue dress becoming green). If you can't do this, then at least try to read in whole scenes.

28

- Set page goals in advance, and check them off to assist managing your progress and when you'll be finished. For example, aim to cover a set number of pages (like 20, 40, or 60) a day.
- Zoom your focus to the line level. You are less concerned now with the story, and more with the expression from one line to the next. (Proofreading is a closer zoom again, looking at mistakes in spelling, grammar and punctuation. You can miss the flow of the sentences at this level, which is why copyediting and proofreading are best kept separate).
- If you are a hopeless tinkerer, and you get stuck going over and over something, try doing your copyedit on paper. Having to erase can dampen the habit.

Proof your manuscript

The final stage, once the copyedit is done, is to proofread. By this stage you'll be so familiar with the manuscript that you'll easily miss mistakes – it's a good idea to have someone else read it. And it does need to be read. Certainly, run your word processor's spellchecker, and consider using a consistency checker (like PerfectIt, which will check you have consistently used capitalisation, hyphenation, and many other non-spelling related issues), but a human also needs to read through it. Fix any errors in the manuscript.

Rinse and repeat if needed

In reality, as an author I often do the PAPER process more than once. Often, once after the first draft to fix things I know are wrong before it goes to my beta readers - though this is usually only a few issues. Then again after the beta readers, but before submitting to the publisher. Then, once again when the publisher gives me their structural report. This simply reflects an iterative process of refinement that many novels go through in response to different kinds of input. The PAPER process makes each straightforward, and I learn things for next time. You may find your novel needs more than one edit in the same way.

When you've edited according to all the appropriate feedback, the novel really is done. Congratulations!

What now?

If publishing is your goal, the rest of the Review steps support submitting, or self-publishing.

Find a publisher or agent, or self-publish

Most people are going through this process because they want to publish their novel. Once you've edited, though, it's a good idea to take a hard look at the book and decide if you *want* to publish it. Sometimes, you might not. Here are some reasons why:

- You feel that even after the edit, you're not happy with the book. Sometimes, your vision was too ambitious for your current skill level. My first novel is still in my drawer because I don't have the skills yet to write it properly. One day I will, but it was in no shape to go out into the world when I first wrote it.

- You have written a genre you don't intend to write again. This might not be a problem for self-publishing, but if you're looking for an agent or traditional publisher, you really need consistency. If you have written a Regency romance novel, but from now on you want to write crime novels, then it's best if you put the romance away and start submitting crime novels.

Assuming you do want to publish, others have written more exhaustively on how to find an agent or publisher, but here is a short list:

- Many publishers have some kind of open submission system – your local writers' centre may even have a publication that lists them. Agents, similarly, may be open or closed. Check their websites. In either case, follow their directions exactly for what and how they want you to submit.

- Other avenues are to enter competitions with publication or introductions to agents or publishers in the prizes; go to industry events where agents and publishers are and talk to them (not just about your novel – aim to make genuine connections over shared interests – you both like books!); apply for development programs;

or book a pitching session at a conference. Join your local writers' centre or genre-specific association to find out about these kinds of opportunities.

If you are self-publishing, you need to identify what platform you'll go through (e.g. Amazon, Smashwords, Draft2Digital), become familiar with their formatting requirements, and organise any marketing and promotion you intend to do.

Assemble marketing tools

Once you know where you will submit (or publish) you will need to assemble some tools to complement your manuscript.

Pitch

A pitch is typically a single sentence (two max) that captures the premise of the story. The idea is that it allows you to quickly tell someone else the idea, without umming and ahhhing and explaining the whole story in excruciating detail.

There are two forms – the direct premise:

- A billionaire businessman falls in love with a prostitute during a week of a critical business deal in Los Angeles. (*Pretty Woman*)
- A vengeful 1890s magician sacrifices everything to best his greatest rival in performing the ultimate illusion. (*The Prestige*)
- A group of fiercely competitive British riders compete—both in the ring and in bed—to be the ultimate horseman in the 1970s European showjumping circuit. (*Riders* by Jilly Cooper)
- A young city doctor takes a temporary job in a remote town to heal her professional confidence and falls in love with a determined heir to a failing cattle station. (My first novel, *Ryders Ridge*)

Or, the combo premise (makes use of existing well-known story tropes – just be careful where you use these):

- Die Hard, in the White House (*Olympus Has Fallen* or *White House Down*)
- Pride and Prejudice and Zombies (which is actually the title, by Seth Grahame-Smith)
- The British Iron Age with Dragons (my as yet unpublished historical fantasy, The White Lance)

If you intend to publish, try to write one of these pitches for your book – you can use it in a cover letter to a publisher or agent, or in your description if self-publishing. This section is not exhaustive on how to write a good one, so you'll need to read more if you're unsure.

Blurb

Blurbs are the things you read on the back of a novel. They are usually only one or two paragraphs, and an expanded version of the premise (it needs to detail the characters, the situation they're in, and what challenges they'll face). Critically, a blurb will usually only hint at the events in the second half of the book, and it NEVER reveals the ending.

Synopsis

A synopsis is a much more structured approach to the story, and if you've done your job right in structuring your narrative, a synopsis falls together reasonably easily. If you have no guidelines (sometimes publishers will ask for a 4-page synopsis, which is painful), then ONE PAGE is the best rule. A suggested structure is:

- An introductory paragraph that captures the premise – often very similar to what might be at the start of a blurb.
- A paragraph that outlines the beginning
- A paragraph (maybe 2) for the middle
- A paragraph for the end of the story, where the type of ending is given explicitly or strongly hinted at (there's no such thing as spoilers in a synopsis).
- A short sentence at the end which gives the genre, and word count.

Make use of joining words like "meanwhile", "at the same time", "despite this", etc., to bridge across what is very summarised material. Avoid the temptation to explain too much, even terms special to your world. Try to rely on context and create an atmosphere. You do not have to render the whole story in the synopsis – it is a selling tool. Above all, you want a sense of the story arc. You will lose this if you try to cram too much into the synopsis.

Writing a synopsis is a non-trivial exercise, and again, this section is not exhaustive on how to do it.

Summary

The Review step is the final stage.

- Once the structural edit is done, read the manuscript to catch any remaining issues, and copyedit to improve the language style.
- Finally, proofread just looking for mistakes in grammar, spelling and formatting.
- When seeking publication, prepare tools to help sell – a pitch and a synopsis are good to have. Target a publisher who is appropriate for your work, and always follow guidelines for submission.

Where to from here?

We could do a whole book talking about the philosophy of writing and how it fits into your wider life. But all I want to say now is this:

- Full-time writing is often a writer's goal, but ask yourself if that's what you really want, and if it's achievable. You do need to be honest with yourself about what full-time writing would mean (such as being able to produce at least one book a year). Most writers combine writing with other work.

- Achieving publication can be a long road. Keep at it. Talent is cheap; persistence is rare.

- Also, if you want to be a writer, you need to write the next book. Don't wait while your last project is doing the rounds in the world. Move on and achieve a healthy separation from your last project by getting into your next.

Good luck.

Appendix A. Glossary

Editing plan	An ordered, organised set of instructions on what to edit. It includes a list of problems with solutions, and the solutions mapped specifically into the novel's scenes.
Problem list	The initial list of issues that need fixing in the novel. This is a rough, unordered list with items added as they are identified.
Scene	Scenes are the basic building blocks of the story. If you aren't sure what that means (no shame), take down a favourite book from your shelf. Find chapter 1, and look at the block of text between the start and where you first find a break (indicated by either a dinkus, or a large space). That's a scene. The next scene follows until the next break, and so on. Grasping the scene and its functions is critical because your edit will be driven by scenes – a novel is nothing more than a sequence of scenes, one after the other (it is not, for example, what is written in a synopsis or blurb). We can only edit what appears in scenes. Here's what you need to know: • Scene breaks or dinkuses show where scenes end and begin. • A scene has its own structure – beginning/middle/end – a structure in miniature to the whole story. • It is a "chunk" of story, the smallest part of the story that makes sense on its own. • It must move the story forward. • It should make it clear to the reader where and when they are, within the first few paragraphs. • Generally, we experience a scene from only one point-of-view (max two).

	• Scenes are generally arranged in chapters. The number of scenes per chapter, and the length of scenes, depend a lot on genre, but there should be some kind of natural rhythm to the grouping.
Scene list	A text list of all the scenes in the novel, in order, including: the chapter and scene number (which forms a unique identifier for each scene), a short description, and other information useful to the writer. This may include the setting, the time/date, and subplots involved.
Time map	A graphical representation of the novel in time. Typically, it's a calendar with the scene numbers (3a, 4c, etc.) written in the appropriate days. The calendar could be more or less detailed depending on the book. For example, a thriller that takes place over a single week might use a calendar where each day is broken down into hours so that the scene placements can be more precise.

Appendix B. PAPER editing process summary

Prepare

- Read the manuscript from beginning to end. As you go, compile the *scene list* and *time map* to record the book as it truly is.

- (optional) Identify your genre, other similar works, and what makes this book stand out

- Format your manuscript to industry standards.

Analyse

- Examine your *scene list* and *time map* for structural problems, and write them on the *problem list*. Record possible solutions if they arise, but focus on the problems.

- Read through the manuscript from beginning to end. As you go, write any structural problems on the *problem list*. Again, record possible solutions if they arise, but focus on the problems.

Plan

- Group the issues on the *problem list* in ways meaningful for you. Write the organised problems into the *editing plan*.

- Come up with specific, directed and compatible solutions for each problem. Write these into the *editing plan*.

- Map all the solutions into the manuscript, using the *scene list* and *time map*, and note the scenes in the *editing plan*.

Execute

- Rank each problem in the *editing plan* as easy, medium or hard.

- Work through your *editing plan*, one issue at a time, making the changes in the scenes. Cross off each item as you do it until they are all done.

Review

- Read the edited manuscript to catch any small, outstanding issues.

- Copyedit.

- Proofread. Consider using a consistency checker to ensure consistent hyphenation, capitalisation and spelling.

- Write any materials needed for submission, such as a pitch, blurb or synopsis. Refer to information gathered in *Preparation* to help with query letters.

- Submit to an agent, publisher, or self-publish.

Appendix C. Example scene list and time map

Scene list (from an early draft of *Crystal Creek*)

Ch	Scene	POV	Setting	Description	Subplots		
					Aunt	Katie	John
1	A	Christina	PA hosp	Christina struggles with surgery exam, meet other students and Katie		X	
	B	Christina	C's BNE house	Christina confronts housemate, then goes to the mountain			
	C	Christina	C's BNE house	Christina discovers her next placement has fallen through			
	D	Christina	C's BNE house	Christina organises a place with the army, & calls aunt to help	X		X
2	A	Aiden	Townsville	Aiden and Travers out diving; Travers is hiding something			
	B	Aiden	Townsville	Aiden at work; padre re-appears. Message from his sister			
3	A	Christina	Harriet's house	Christina arrives in Townsville, checks out Aunt's house			X
	B	Christina	Clinic	Christina's first day in the clinic - out of place; Katie shows up unexpectedly		X	
	C	Christina	Clinic	Christina meets Travers, they do ECGs. Katie and C make friends		X	
... and so on ...							

Corresponding time map

Each chapter and scene from above is used to show the scene in time, below.

Week	Mon	Tue	Wed	Thu	Fri	Sat	Sun
1					1a	1b 1c	1d
2	2a 2b						3a
3	3b 3c						

... and so on ...

Appendix D. Manuscript formatting guide

Note: You can also access a Word copy of this guide through my website, http://tinyurl.com/j4j7k9t.

Page intentionally blank to allow manuscript example to begin on an odd page ...

Manuscript Formatting

Charlotte Nash

Chapter 1

The goal of manuscript formatting is to be unobtrusive: setting out your story in such a way that it can speak for itself, without the text layout distracting the reader. In the publishing industry, professionals are used to reading manuscripts that look a particular way. Unless submission guidelines direct you specifically otherwise, stick to these guidelines.

#

Always use Times New Roman if you can (or another similar serif font if you can't), 12 pt, double spaced. Use 3 cm margins. Use plain chapter and section headings.

Indent each paragraph by 1 cm, left justify the text, and do not put extra space between paragraphs. First paragraphs in a new section can be unindented if desired.

It's best to learn how to use your word processor's styles, so that these formats occur automatically. You can find a video on how to do this at: https://www.youtube.com/watch?v=n-6_FTy2dLY. Avoid tabbing the start of each new paragraph, for example, and turn off smart quotes (which suffer reversal problems) in favour of "straight quotes".

Separate scenes with a hash, or a large white space (but use a hash if you are indenting your first paragraphs).

In the header, put your word count aligned left, and your name, title and page number aligned right, as shown. At the end, write END so that the reader knows there is nothing missing. You can make a separate cover page with just the title and your byline, or simply begin the first page part-way down, rolling straight into Chapter 1. It's often a good idea to include a different header on the first page, giving your address and other contact details in the left header, and the word count in the right. The other pages should then follow the format shown on this document.

When you save your file, make sure it's in a format that will be readily accessible. RTF and DOC are usually safe.

#

Avoid at all costs: fancy fonts, pictures, tables, text boxes, and file formats that make the text difficult to access (PDF, PAGES).

Italics are done just like that; the only exception is if you're using `Courier, in which case, underline` instead. Avoid underlining in Times.

Chapter 2

You will find some markets want variations – Courier font, 1.5 line spacing – so check carefully before submitting. But, if there are no guidelines, you won't annoy a busy editor if you use this plain, well-known style. Happy writing.

END

Appendix E. Basic analysis questions

Using your scene list and time map, examine:

- **Premise** – does your story have a sufficiently defined problem for a central character/s, which is present in the beginning and resolved somehow in the end?
- **Structure** – does your story have a beginning, middle, end, and turning points in between?
- **Setting** – do you have repetitions of scene setting that add nothing?
- **Pace** – do you have repetitions of introspective or action scenes with nothing to break up the rhythm?
- **Character viewpoint** – do you have too many, too few or an imbalance of viewpoints to serve the story you're trying to tell?

Now, as you read through the manuscript, examine:

- **Premise** – does the first chapter clearly establish expectations of the story for the reader, without extraneous guff?
- **Primary characters** – is the character defined by their relationship to the world and other characters? Are they interesting enough to follow?
    - o **Drivers and reactions** – do characters have believable internal drives and realistic reactions? Are those drives and reactions evident in their thoughts and actions?
    - o **Arc** – do the characters change in some way in response to the events of the novel? Is this change evident in their thoughts and actions?
    - o **Viewpoint** – do we see the story through the right sets of eyes?
- **Secondary characters** – do the secondary characters all have a clear function? Any repetition? Are they all defined as their own person? Any clichés? Any overshadowing the main cast?
- **Context and setting** – Do the characters always behave believably according to the context? Does the context help to maintain those

characters in the central conflict? Are all the settings consistent in their physical description?

- **Pace** – Are there boring scenes that could be cut or summarised? Or interesting events mentioned in passing that could be shown?
- **Consistency** – are the 'world rules' the same throughout the story? Are there any problems with the timeline?
- **Theme** – is a theme present? Is it under or overdone?
- **Tone** – is the tone of the story always appropriate to its genre, audience and the story events?

Appendix F. Basic solution prompts

Primary characters

If your main characters are uninteresting, ask:

- What foibles or problems do they have that many of us also have? (relatability)
- What qualities or opportunities do they have that many of us might wish for? (aspiration)
- What is at stake for them if they fail? If it isn't life or death (physical, emotional, professional or psychological) then perhaps the problem is too minor for a novel.

Secondary characters

- If you have clichés or stereotypes, play the antagonist game. This is where you imagine the secondary character is a hero in their own story. What kind of person would they be then? What would motivate them?
- If a character is too mysterious, ask what drives them and look for a place to reveal that drive.
- Look for ways to delete secondary characters with repetitive functions, or combine them into one character.

Pace

If the story is slow or dull:

- Is there too much introspection or description? Cut!
- Are characters too passive? Can you give them action rather than reaction?
- Does the character have something to do, or are they waiting around? If so, can you cut? Or, create a new event that would add pressure?

If the story has become unrelentingly fast (too much is happening too quickly):

- How long since we last understood how the character feels – about the events, or in their body? Can you add introspection to modulate the pace?
- Can we clearly visualise where everyone is, or do you have white space? Can you add a descriptive scene, or insert beats of description within your existing scenes?

Conflict

If the characters persist in conflict illogically, could the context change to make them stay there?

Context/setting

Do you have parts of the setting that are difficult to visualise? Or parts of the narrative where the characters are in what feels like white space?

- For small settings (rooms, buildings or villages) draw a map to orient features. Address every sense: What can you see? What can you smell? Taste? Touch? Hear?
- For a whole civilisation – address PERSIA (politics, economics, religion, social, intellectual, artistic).

Disorientation

Check the beginning of each scene. Within the first two paragraphs, do we know where we are? When? Whose head we are in?

Appendix G. Example editing plan

Below shows an open double-page spread in a notebook. The "problem" is numbered, in bold, on the left. Below are the solution/s that solve that problem. On the right, each solution is mapped into the manuscript with scene numbers and any notes of what to change - the level of detail can suit what the writer needs.

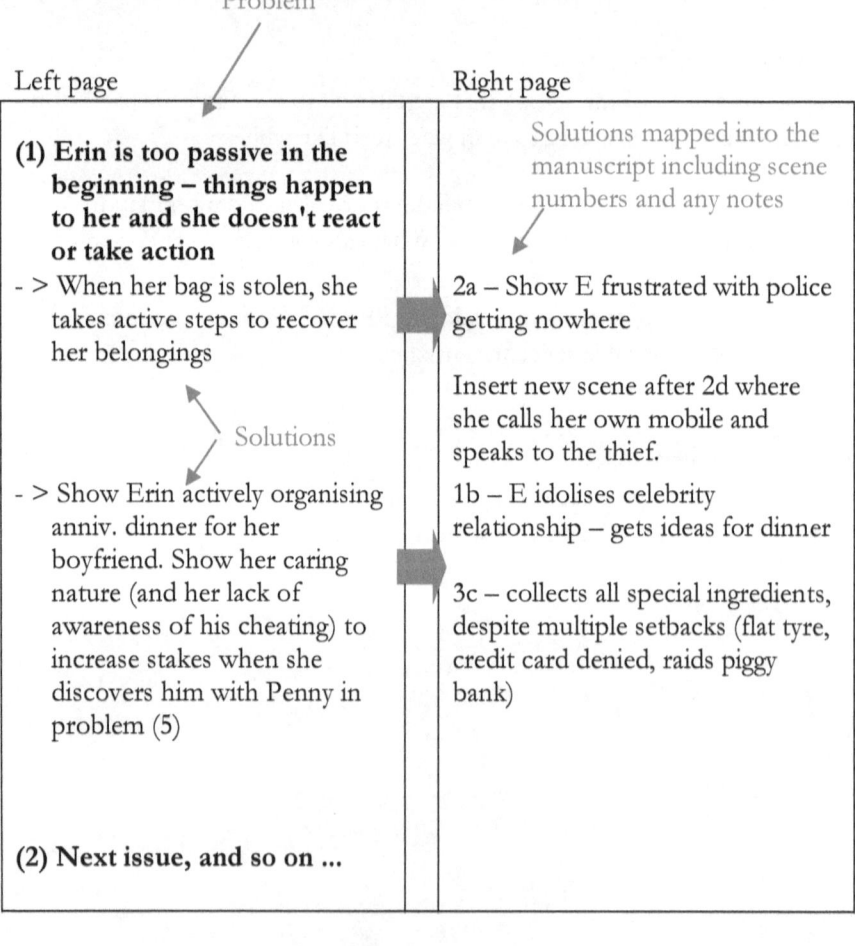

Problem

Left page

(1) Erin is too passive in the beginning – things happen to her and she doesn't react or take action

- > When her bag is stolen, she takes active steps to recover her belongings

Solutions

- > Show Erin actively organising anniv. dinner for her boyfriend. Show her caring nature (and her lack of awareness of his cheating) to increase stakes when she discovers him with Penny in problem (5)

(2) Next issue, and so on ...

Right page

Solutions mapped into the manuscript including scene numbers and any notes

2a – Show E frustrated with police getting nowhere

Insert new scene after 2d where she calls her own mobile and speaks to the thief.

1b – E idolises celebrity relationship – gets ideas for dinner

3c – collects all special ingredients, despite multiple setbacks (flat tyre, credit card denied, raids piggy bank)

Appendix H. Rough time guide

This table is a guide to how long it takes me to perform various writing and editing tasks for novels. In this case, a novel is 90,000–100,000 words. I would class myself as a reasonably fast writer, and a medium-paced editor.

Task	Full-time	Part-time
First draft	2 – 6 weeks of writing days 3 – 14 weeks total[1]	6 – 14 weeks of writing days 17 – 30 weeks total[2]
Structural edit	2 weeks flat out 3 – 4 weeks comfortable	4 weeks flat out
Copyedit – my edit	4 – 5 days[3]	2 weeks
Copyedit – checking another person's copyedit	1.5 weeks flat out 2 – 3 weeks comfortable	
Proofs	3 days flat out 4 – 5 days comfortable	

---

[1] I have good data on my novel writing, as I kept detailed spreadsheets for each (full-time data is based on 5 novels). Total time here means the calendar period it took to write – even though this is "full-time" writing, some days I had other work to do (for example, a copyedit on another book), and I often didn't write on weekends. Writing days means the actual number of days I wrote the novel, even though they were spread over a longer time.

[2] Part-time data is based on 4 novels. These were written earlier in my career, when I was still working full-time.

[3] Takes 3 days to mark-up the hard-copy manuscript, and 1–2 days to enter the changes into the soft copy.